The Power Of Holy Spirit

By

Dr. Kenton Edward Emmanuel Connor

COPYRIGHT@2020

TABLE OF CONTENT

THE HOLINESS THAT COMES THROUGH FIRE

COPYRIGHT

INTRODUCTION

In the Word of God (the Bible), the Holy Spirit is called various names – the Holy Ghost, the Paraclete, the Comforter, the Helper, Breath of the Almighty God, Power of the Highest, Eternal Spirit, Spirit of the Father, Spirit of Christ, Spirit of the Son, Spirit of life and so on and so forth.

When He had almost completed His mission on earth, our Lord and Saviour Jesus Christ told His Apostles in **John 14:15-17,** "If you love me, you will obey my commandments. I will ask the Father (God) and He will give you another Helper, who will stay with you forever. He is the Spirit who reveals the truth about God.

The world cannot receive Him, because it cannot see Him. But you know Him, because He remains with you and is in you."

Jesus was referring to the Holy Spirit here and He made a clear distinction that only those who obey His commandments would

receive the Holy Spirit who will reveal the truth about God.

Jesus goes further to say in **John 14:18-21**, "When I go, you will not be left all alone; I will come back to you. In a little while the world will see me no more, but you will see me; and because I live, you also will live. When that day comes, you will know that I am in the Father and that you are in me, just as I am in you.

Whoever accepts my commandments and obeys them is the one who loves me. My Father will love whoever love me; I too will love him and reveal myself to him."

Again Jesus is referring to the Holy Trinity (God the Father, Himself, God the Son and God the Holy Spirit).

We clearly infer from Jesus' statement that anyone who does not obey His commandments does not love Him and His Father (God) loves those who obey Jesus' commands and Jesus loves and reveals Himself to them.

So the Holy Spirit of God only comes to those who obey Jesus's commandments. Jesus fulfilled His promise of the Holy Spirit to His Apostles on Pentecost Day, ten days after He ascended to Heaven **(Acts 2:1-12).** The Holy Spirit has guided the Body of Christ (the Church) through the ages, revealing the truth about God till this present day.

We see this in Jesus' words to His Apostles in **John 16:12-15,** "I have much more to tell you, but now it would be too much for you to bear. When, however, the Spirit comes, who reveals the truth about God, He will lead you into all truth. He will not speak on His own authority, but He will speak of what He hears, and will tell you of things to come.

He will give me glory, because He will take what I say and tell it to you. All that my Father has is mine; that is why I said that the Spirit will take what I give Him and tell it to you."

Indeed, anyone who sincerely obeys Jesus' commandments would have the promise of

the Holy Spirit as a guide to the truth about God. Those who disobey Jesus' commandments cannot have the promise of the Holy Spirit. These are the ones Jesus refers to as the world that cannot see or receive the Holy Spirit.

How does a person know if he or she has the Holy Spirit in him or her? Is it by claiming to know God or Jesus Christ? The Word of God clarifies this issue in **Galatians 5:16-26,** "What I say is this: let the Holy Spirit direct your lives, and you will not satisfy the desires of human nature.

For what our human nature wants is opposed to what the Spirit wants, and what the Spirit wants is opposed to what our human nature wants. These two are enemies, and this means that you cannot do what you want to do. If the Spirit leads you, then you are not subject to the law.

What human nature does is ⬜uite plain. It shows itself in immoral, filthy and indecent actions; in worship of idols and witchcraft. People become enemies and they fight;

they become jealous, angry and ambitious. They separate into parties and groups; they are envious, get drunk, have orgies, and do other things like these. I warn you now as I have before: those who do these things will not possess the Kingdom of God.

But the Spirit produces love, joy, peace, patience, kindness, goodness, faithfulness, humility, and self-control. There is no law against such things as these. And those who belong to Christ Jesus have put to death their human nature with all its passions and desires. The Spirit has given us life; He must also control our lives. We must not be proud or irritate one another or be jealous of one another."

These □ualities in the preceding paragraph are the fruits of the Holy Spirit that manifest in those who love Christ Jesus and obey His commandments and whom the Holy Spirit will come into their lives.

Dear reader, it is important to note here that our Lord Jesus Christ also loves those who do not obey His commands, but the love He has for them is what made Him die on the cross for mankind's sins to reconcile mankind to God over 2,013 years ago. Jesus, who is God and the creator of everything in Heaven and on earth knows the beginning from the end.

He knows that anyone here on earth who is not obeying His commands is living a dangerous life and does not have the Holy Spirit as a guide to the truth about God. If such person dies and leaves this earth in sin, that person's soul ends up in hell FOREVER without any other chance for repentance. The chance for repentance is only here on earth and NOW when we are still alive.

ONLY those who obey Jesus' commandments would make it to Heaven when they depart this world because the Holy Spirit will always be with them here on earth to lead them to the truth about God as Jesus promised and as continues to happen till today.

Jesus created hell for Satan and his demons but many people continue to sin by disobeying Jesus' commands and die to end

up in eternal torment in hell with Satan. A lot of souls die every single day in sin and are presently in hell undergoing torment.

Jesus continues to weep daily because of this very sad truth and in His love and mercy as our Father He has taken several people to show them the realities of hell with perished souls there in eternal torment and heaven with its astounding beauty and returned these witnesses to earth with a warning to mankind to repent of sins and turn to Him (Jesus) as the ONLY guarantee of getting to heaven.

Satan now continues to laugh since he and his demons are presently tormenting the souls of those who died in sin in hell. Satan will get his own punishment when hell and death are cast into the lake burning with fire and sulphur, which is the second death **(Revelation 21:8).**

HOLY SPIRIT POWER!

A Christian friend came over asking that several of us pray for her. Despite doing all the "right" Christian things, she had been entertaining doubts about her faith.

In the course of our prayer, as I was reminding her of what Scripture says about how God sees her, in a gruff tone of voice, with furrowed brow, she scolded me, speaking in the third person, "She doesn't deserve it! She doesn't deserve it!" In a couple of hours, by the Power of the Holy Spirit, she was free from demonic bondage with a total change of countenance and has, since then, moved forward with marriage and ministry.

On an Easter Sunday morning, as I was attending a Baptist church service, a man sat praying, head bowed, as the congregation headed for the exits. I approached him and asked if I might pray. He ignored me. I laid my hand on his shoulder to pray. The moment I touched him, he bolted upright, began swaying like a cobra about to strike, and started

growling as he pointed, "I hate him! I hate her! I hate this church!"

My attempts to minister were interrupted by well-meaning people asking if he needed medication or asking if they should call an ambulance. When the man became unable to open his mouth to speak, I commanded the spirit to release his tongue. Instantly, he was able to understand me then and speak intelligibly in response to me. I told him I was available for further ministry by the Holy Spirit but it was obvious there was no faith present to deliver him at that moment. I made him aware that, until he got help, this WAS his Christian life and he WOULD experience these manifestations again. I left only to be bombarded with Questions throughout the week by those who were there.

I could write many personal encounters like these, moments when the Holy Spirit took control, flushed out an unsuspecting demon, healed, delivered, set free or came through with a vision, word of wisdom or word of knowledge. He is no respecter of

persons; the gifts He has shared with me, He wants to share with you.

Question is, are you willing? Do you desire more?

WE ARE SPIRIT BEINGS HAVING AN EARTHLY EXPERIENCE. WE ARE ALIENS.

We have no permanent citizenship in this world. Though we are citizens of the United States, the reality is that, as a Christian, our citizenship is in Heaven **(Phil 3:20).** As the book of Hebrews says, "Here we have no lasting city, but we seek the city which is to come" **(Heb. 13:14)** For we are strangers before thee, and sojourners, as were all our fathers: our days on the earth are as a shadow, and there is none abiding. **(1 Chron 29;15)**

WE ARE ENAGED IN A SPIRITUAL WAR - a term not found in Scripture, but the concept is taught. Mankind is caught in the midst of a spiritual war with the holy God and His angels on one side and the evil Satan and his demons on the other.

(2 Cor 10:3-5) "For though we live in the world, we do not wage war as the world does. The weapons we fight with are not the weapons of the world. On the contrary, they have divine power to demolish strongholds. We demolish arguments and every pretension that sets itself up against the knowledge of God, and we take captive every thought to make it obedient to Christ."

(Eph 6:11-12) Put on the full armor of God so that you can take your stand against the devil's schemes. For our struggle is not against flesh and blood, but against the rulers, against the authorities, against the powers of this dark world and against the spiritual forces of evil in the heavenly realms.

(Rev 12:7-8) And there was war in heaven. Michael and his angels fought against the dragon, and the dragon and his angels fought back. But he was not strong enough, and they lost their place in heaven. The great dragon was hurled down--that ancient serpent called the devil,

or Satan, who leads the whole world astray. He was hurled to the earth, and his angels with him.

IF WE RESIST THE DEVIL, HE WILL FLEE

(James 4: 7) Resist the devil, and he will flee from you.

WE DO NOT HAVE THE POWER TO RESIST SATAN ON OUR OWN

(Jude 9) But even the archangel Michael, when he was disputing with the devil about the body of Moses, did not dare to bring a slanderous accusation against him, but said, "The Lord rebuke you!"

TO RESIST THE DEVIL, WE MUST PUT ON THE FULL ARMOR OF GOD

(Eph 6:10-12) Put on the full armor of God so that you can take your stand against the devil's schemes. For our struggle is not against flesh and blood, but against the rulers, against the authorities, against the powers of this dark world and

against the spiritual forces of evil in the heavenly realms. Therefore put on the full armor of God, so that when the day of evil comes, you may be able to stand your ground, and after you have done everything, to stand. Stand firm then, with the belt of truth buckled around your waist, with the breastplate of righteousness in place, and with your feet fitted with the readiness that comes from the gospel of peace. In addition to all this, take up the shield of faith, with which you can extinguish all the flaming arrows of the evil one. Take the helmet of salvation and the sword of the Spirit, which is the word of God. And pray in the Spirit on all occasions with all kinds of prayers and requests. With this in mind, be alert and always keep on praying for all the saints.

Jesus' own mission statement: "He hath sent me to bind up the broken-hearted, to proclaim liberty to the captives, and the opening [of the prison] to them that are bound; to proclaim the year of the Lord's favor." **(Isa 61:1,2)**

GOD ALLOWS TEMPTATIONS, BUT ALWAYS PROVIDES AN ESCAPE

(1 Cor 10:13) No temptation has seized you except what is common to man. And God is faithful; he will not let you be tempted beyond what you can bear. But when you are tempted, he will also provide a way out so that you can stand up under it.

SATAN KNOWS THE SCRIPTURES AND TRIES TO MISUSE THEM

As described in **Matt 4:3-10 and Luke 4:3-12,** during the temptation of Jesus in the wilderness, Satan □uoted Him Scripture several times. Jesus replied each time with additional Scriptures refuting Satan's attempts to take things out of context or only use part of a section.

(Matt 28:19-20, Lk 9:1-2 and 10:1-3).

Too many American Christians have become passive and fearful. Others are satisfied to merely acknowledge the right things and attend church services and

activities. This type of lifestyle is ☐uite different from that which Jesus requires of His followers.

We must preach and teach about the kingdom of God, focus on the doctrine of Christ, heal the sick and set the captives free.

Why is the Holy Spirit referred to as being "holy"?(HOLY: Belonging to, derived from, or associated with a divine power; sacred.) Distinguishes Him from EVIL spirits.

SAD FACTS REGARDING THE CHURCH AND THE HOLY SPIRIT

A majority (61%) agree that the Holy Spirit is a symbol of God's presence or power but is not a living entity. (2001)

Among the segments of the population more likely than others to deny the existence of the Holy Spirit as a living entity are Catholics (73%), non-Christians (68%), and non-whites (68%). (2001)

A majority of all born again Christians reject the existence of the Holy Spirit (52%). (2001)

WHY IS THE HOLY SPIRIT IMPORTANT?

There is no subject more important in Christianity than that of the Holy Spirit. Unless this is properly understood, a large portion of the Bible, and especially the NT, remains unintelligible. On the other hand, a just view of it will do more than a knowledge of any other particular topic to give harmony, clearness, and consistency to what may be learned to all other matters presented in the Word of God.

Despite the importance of knowing the Holy Spirit and His place in the life of a Christian, there is much confusion and superstition in the minds of many people about the Holy Spirit

WHO IS THE HOLY SPIRIT?

1. A person with characteristics

2. NOT, merely an "influence", or "impersonal force" that emanates from God.

3. We should regard the Holy Spirit as a "He", not an "it"!

I. THE HOLY SPIRIT'S PERSONALITY

A. THE HOLY SPIRIT SPEAKS...

1. He "expressly says" that some will depart from the faith - **1 Tim 4:1**

2. The Spirit spoke and gave directions to Philip - **Acts 8:29**

3. He spoke to Peter and gave him charge concerning the Gentiles - **Acts 10:19-20**

4. He spoke to the brethren at Antioch concerning Paul and Barnabas - **Acts 13:1-4**

B. THE HOLY SPIRIT TEACHES...

1. He was to teach the apostles all things - **Jn 14:26**

2. Please note that Jesus consistently refers to the Holy Spirit as "He", not "it" (implying a personal being, not an impersonal force) - **Jn 14:16-**17

C. THE HOLY SPIRIT BEARS WITNESS...

1. He was to testify of Jesus - **Jn 15:26-27**

2. Just as the apostles (who were "personal beings") would bear witness, so also the Holy Spirit

D. THE HOLY SPIRIT GUIDES, HEARS, SPEAKS, TELLS...

1. He would carry on and complete the work started by Jesus - **Jn 16:12-13**

2. Jesus consistently refers to the Holy Spirit as "He"
The Holy Spirit is a real person who came to reside within Jesus Christ's true followers after Jesus rose from the dead and ascended to heaven **(Acts 2).** Jesus told His apostles...

"I will ask the Father, and He will give you another Helper, that He may be with you forever; the Spirit of truth, whom the world cannot receive, because it does not behold Him or know Him, but you know Him because He abides with you, and will be in you. I will not leave you as orphans; I will come to you." **(Jn 14:16-18)**

The Holy Spirit is not a vague, ethereal shadow, nor an impersonal force. He is a person equal in every way with God the Father and God the Son. He is considered to be the third member of the Godhead. Jesus said to His apostles...

"All authority has been given to Me in heaven and on earth. Go therefore and make disciples of all the nations, baptizing them in the name of the Father and the Son and the Holy Spirit, teaching them to observe all that I commanded you; and lo, I am with you always, even to the end of the age." **(Matt 28:18-20)**

God is Father, Son and Holy Spirit. And all the divine attributes ascribed to the Father and the Son are equally ascribed to the

Holy Spirit. When a person becomes born again by believing and receiving Jesus Christ **(Jn 1:12-13; Jn 3:3-21),** God resides in that person through the Holy Spirit **(1Cor 3:16).**

E. THE HOLY SPIRIT'S PRIMARY ROLE

1. He bears "witness" of Jesus Christ and tells people's hearts about the truth of Jesus Christ. **(Jn 15:26, 16:14).**

2. He acts as a Christian's teacher/guide **(1Cor. 2:9-14).**

3. He reveals God's will and God's truth to a Christian. Jesus told His disciples...

"The Helper, the Holy Spirit, whom the Father will send in My name, He will teach you all things, and bring to your remembrance all that I said to you." **(Jn 14:26)**

"When He, the Spirit of truth, comes, He will guide you into all the truth; for He will not speak on His own initiative, but whatever He hears, He will speak; and He

will disclose to you what is to come." **(Jn 16:13)**

4. The Holy Spirit was given to live inside those who believe in Jesus, in order to produce God's character in the life of a believer. In a way that we cannot do on our own, the Holy Spirit will build into our lives love, joy, peace, patience, kindness, goodness, faithfulness, gentleness and self-control **(Gal 5:22-23).** Rather than trying to be loving, patient, kind, God asks us to rely on Him to produce these □ualities in our lives. Thus Christians are told to walk in the Spirit **(Gal 5:25)** and be filled with the Spirit **(Eph 5:18).**

5. The Holy Spirit empowers Christians to perform ministerial duties that promote spiritual growth among Christians **(Rom 12; 1Cor 12; Eph 4).**

6. The Holy Spirit also performs a function for non-Christians as well. He convicts people's hearts of God's truth concerning how sinful we are -- needing God's forgiveness; how righteous Jesus is -- He died in our place, for our sins; and God's

eventual judgment of the world and those who do not know Him **(Jn 16:8-11).** The Holy Spirit tugs on our hearts and minds, asking us to repent and turn to God for forgiveness and a new life.

F. THE HOLY SPIRIT FORBIDS...

1. He prevented Paul and his companions from going into certain areas of Asia - **Acts 16:6-7** This He did by "forbidding" them, and "not permitting" them, despite their initial efforts

G. THE HOLY SPIRIT INTERCEDES...

1. The "Spirit Himself (note Paul's use of the personal pronoun) makes intercession for us" - **Rom 8:26**
2. Just as Christ "also makes intercession for us" - **Rom 8:34** [All these works of the Holy Spirit manifest personality]

II. THE HOLY SPIRIT POSSESSES PERSONAL CHARACTERISTICS

A. HE HAS A MIND...

1. "the mind of the Spirit" - Rom **8:27** This suggests thinking on His own.

B. HE HAS KNOWLEDGE...

1. He "knows the things of God" - **1 Cor 2:11** just as the "spirit of man" (a personal being) knows certain things. He has intellect.

C. HE POSSESSES AFFECTION...

1. Paul speaks of "the love of the Spirit" - **Rom 15:30** When have you known of an "impersonal force" that could love? He has emotion.

D. HE HAS A WILL...

1. "the same Spirit works all these things, distributing to each one individually as He wills" - **1 Cor 12:11** It was the Holy Spirit Who decided what person received which gift. Again, these are all characteristics of a being possessing intelligence and personality.

III. THE HOLY SPIRIT SUFFERS PERSONAL SLIGHTS AND INJURIES

A. HE CAN BE GRIEVED...

1. "do not grieve the Holy Spirit of God" - **Eph 4:30** He can be made sorrowful through our willful neglect

B. HE CAN BE BLASPHEMED...

1. That is, to be spoken evil of, as in attributing His deeds to the works of Satan, the "unpardonable sin" - **Matt 12:31-32**

C. HE CAN BE INSULTED...
1. One who has "trampled the Son of God underfoot" has also "insulted the Spirit of grace" - Heb 10:29 This is done by sinning "willfully" - Heb 10:26

D. HE CAN BE LIED TO...

1. As Ananias and his wife Sapphira were guilty of doing. **Acts 5:3:** "...why has Satan filled your heart to lie to the Holy Spirit...?"

E. HE CAN BE RESISTED...

1. As Stephen charged the Jewish leaders of doing - **Acts 7:51** This they did by resisting the message and persecuting the messengers who were inspired by the Holy Spirit. **Acts 7: 52-53**

In my opinion, much too great an emphasis has been placed on the gift of tongues - so much so that an ungodly caste system of the haves and have-not's has developed in some groups - despite the promise of Scripture that you shall receive POWER (NOT tongues) when the Spirit comes upon you; power to be a witness (literally, a martyr). Request my study entitled "Speaking of speaking in tongues."

HOW TO STOP SINNING AND START LIVING A HOLY LIFE PLEASING TO GOD

God has called Christians to live a holy life that glorifies Him. "Be ye holy; for I am holy" **(1 Peter 1:16).** You are a spirit, you have a soul and you live in a body. As a Christian, your spirit is perfect and holy, born of God. However, your soul (mind, will and emotions) is not perfect and holy because it has not been made new like your spirit. Your soul is still motivated by sinful desires, strongholds of the mind.

Your soul must be renewed and made holy by a special process called sanctification. Sanctification means being made holy. That is to be your goal, to sanctify your soul, making it conform to God's highest standard of conduct, holiness.

With God's help, you will use four powerful weapons to tear down the sin producing strongholds of the mind: God's Word, praying in tongues, worship and sowing and reaping. We'll start with God's Word.

God's Word

The Word of God is like a giant divine wrecking ball that can destroy any destructive stronghold of the mind. "For the word of God is □uick, and powerful, and sharper than any two edged sword, piercing even to the dividing asunder of soul and spirit, and of the joints and marrow, and is a discerner of the thoughts and intents of the heart" **(Hebrew 4:12).**

To release the power in God's Word to attack and defeat the unholy strongholds in your mind, the Word must become rhema. I will explain. Rhema is a Greek word which means "the spoken Word of God" and is filled with faith and power that produces results. Example: Jesus spoke one rhema word to Peter, "Come." And just on that one faith filled word, Peter walked on the water. Logos is a Greek word that means "the written Word of God." It has power, but not the instant dynamic power of the rhema Word.

The logos will become a rhema word when you spend enough time meditating it. Meditation of the Word of God is simply taking a scripture and thinking on it, muttering it, speaking it, declaring it, visualizing it until it becomes real in your heart. The Holy Spirit is the Spirit of Revelation and He is the one who will breath life on the logos and cause it to become the rhema.

So, this is what you do. I have seven scripture based declarations below that you will daily think on, mutter, speak, declare and visualize (seeing yourself living a holy life, victorious over sin). I suggest spending at least a half hour a day doing this. The more time you give to this, the Quicker the results.

Scripture Based Declarations

1. I have hidden your Word in my heart that I might not sin against you **(Psalm119:11).**
2. My old sinful man was crucified with Christ so I am no longer controlled and

dominated by the sin nature **(Romans 6:6).**

3. It is impossible for me to sin because my old sinful man died on the cross with Christ and he that is dead is free from sin **(Romans 6:7).**

4. I reckon myself dead to all sin, but alive unto God through Jesus Christ my Lord. Praise God, I am dead to sin but alive onto God **(Romans 6:11)!**

5. Because I am dead to sin, sin no longer has dominion over me **(Romans 6:11,14).**

6. I am a new creature in Christ and old things are passed away and all things have become new, therefore I no longer sin, but walk in holiness **(2 Corinthians 5:17).**

7. I am born of incorruptible seed by the word of God, therefore I am holy and I cannot sin **(1 Peter 1:23).**

Praying in Tongues

The Holy Spirit is our Helper and He can intercede for you when you spend time privately praying in tongues. You see, when you pray in tongues He prays through you to God concerning any harmful and sinful things in your life. "Likewise the Spirit also helpeth our infirmities: for we know not what we should pray for as we ought: but the Spirit itself maketh intercession for us with groanings which cannot be uttered" **(Romans 8:26).**

Spend at least a half hour praying in tongues everyday. The more time you spend praying in tongues, the better. Don't believe in speaking and praying in tongues? Read **Acts 2:4** and **Jude 20-21.** Never been filled with the Holy Spirit with the evidence of speaking in tongues? Ask God the Father in Jesus' name to fill you with the Holy Spirit with the evidence of speaking in tongues. Ask in faith and then let 'er rip.

Worshipping God Daily in Spirit and Truth

Worshipping God daily in spirit and truth will bring about a manifestation of God's presence in your life that will help produce in you the sanctified life and will draw you closer to Him. He is seeking those that will worship Him on a daily basis. "But the hour cometh, and now is, when the true

worshippers shall worship the Father in spirit and truth: for the Father seeketh such to worship him" **(John 4:23).** The more time you spend doing this, the better.

Set aside a time each day and begin thanking the Lord Jesus Christ for what He has done for you through His death and resurrection. Thank Him for your salvation. Thank Him for redeeming you from sin, sickness, disease, poverty and the second death which is the lake of fire. Thank Him that you are blessed with faithful Abraham because you have put your faith in Christ and the Gospel. Then begin praising Him for who He is. Praise Him for His glory, power, love, wisdom, knowledge, peace, joy, honor, riches, blessing and holiness.

Finally, begin to worship Him, telling Him how much you love Him. Telling Him how awesome and glorious He is. Tell Him you magnify Him. You glorify Him. Be in awe of His holiness. If you have never worshipped God like this before, start out with just a few minutes of thanksgiving and praise. Then spend fifteen minutes worshipping Him. Eventually you will want to stretch

your worship time to a half hour or more. What happens in this sanctifying process? God begins to manifest His presence and you are changed on the inside which will eventually manifest outwardly from you. "Draw nigh to God, and he will draw nigh to you" **(James 4:8a).**

Sowing and Reaping

There is great power in a financial seed sown in faith. Your tithe (10% of your income) takes care of the operating expenses of your local church. God honors your tithe seed planted and gives you a harvest of fulfilling the operating expenses of your home. Your offering is anything above your tithe. This is what you do to get a harvest of freedom from sin. Name your offering seed "freedom from sin and holy living." Sow that financial seed into good soil and expect to receive your harvest.

Good soil is a ministry that is winning souls for God and it is prospering financially because it believes and operates in God's dynamic financial system of sowing and reaping. Your own local church might be

good soil if they are winning souls to Christ and believe and operate in God's superior financial system of sowing and reaping. Your offering does not take the place of your tithe, so make sure you sow both your tithes and offerings or you will be robbing God according to **Malachi 3:8.**

There are a number of ministries I will recommend for you to sow your offering seed: Ever Increasing Word Ministries, Jesse Duplantis Ministries, Bill Winston Ministries and Kenneth Copeland Ministries. These are all good soils for your seed sown and will produce harvests if you sow in faith consistently. "Consistently" means you are a consistent sower of your tithes and offerings. It is not a "one shot" thing.

Well, there you have it. Daily meditate God's Word, daily pray in tongues, daily worship the Lord Jesus Christ and consistently name your seed sown in good soil to reap a harvest of holy living. Do this faithfully and your bondage to sin should be over and your life of holiness should become a reality, well pleasing to God.

One thing I did not mention. The fire of God. One hundred and twenty disciples of Jesus were in the upper room when the fire of God fell. What did the fire of God do? The fire of God burned out the carnal things in their life, things like fear, sin and unbelief. If you are serious about being used of God mightily, click on "Fire of God" below.

Financial three step plans, money making formulas and sowing and reaping scriptures can all be well and good, but if you have a poverty stronghold lodged and hidden in your mind, you may never enter your earthly wealthy place. If you feel you might have a poverty mental stronghold keeping you from your wealthy place and you want to be set free, then click on "Free from a Poverty Mental Stronghold" below.

BE FILLED WITH THE HOLY SPIRIT

Drawing closer to God and experiencing His very Presence and power is the result of the application of certain spiritual principles over and over again, being consistent and persistent in our pursuit of God and His plan and purpose for our lives.

We draw closer to God through spending time with Him in His Word, the Holy Bible, and in prayer.

One of the most awesome ways to pray is in the Holy Spirit. By this, I am referring to praying in the language of the Spirit, which is known in the Bible as praying in tongues.

I know that this is a subject of much controversy. Many people do not understand the value of praying to God in this manner. And because of a lack of understanding of the subject of being filled with the blessed Holy Spirit, which is accompanied by the ability to speak to God in a supernatural language, people have

been robbed of their inheritance in Christ, and a marvelous manner in which to speak to God, spirit to Spirit.

I believe that the subject of the infilling of the Holy Spirit needs to be explain simply and clearly, so that its relevance and necessity can be appreciated and valued.

The mighty baptism with the Holy Spirit, which is the same thing as being filled with the Holy Spirit, is not the same experience as salvation. It is rather a gift from the Father, after we are saved or born again.

Someone may ask, Do I need to be filled with the Holy Spirit to go to Heaven? The answer is no.

All a person needs to go to Heaven is salvation through the shed blood of the Lord Jesus Christ. When you give your heart to Christ, as Lord and Savior, you are washed from sin in the precious blood of Christ. You are born again, born from above, made a new creature in Christ Jesus, and you, as a child of the Living God, should the Lord Jesus come, stand

ready to go with Him, provided you remain in Him.

You do not need to be filled with the Holy Spirit, speaking with other tongues, to get to Heaven. The mighty baptism with the Holy Spirit is to empower you to be an effective witness of the Lord Jesus Christ on the earth.

Well, someone may ask, are you implying that every Christian who is not filled with the Holy Spirit, speaking in other tongues, does not have the Holy Ghost?

No, that would be wrong as well. Every person who has received the Lord Jesus Christ as Lord and Savior, has the Holy Spirit living within. He is the personal representative of Jesus Christ within the believer. The Holy Bible teaches that He is within us as our pledge and guarantee of our new bodies when the Lord Jesus Christ comes for His people.

He is Christ in us, the hope of glory. Every Christian has the Holy Spirit within. But not every Christian is filled with the Holy Spirit

and empowered supernaturally to work for the Lord.

A car may have gas in it. But that does not mean it is filled with gas, does it? Likewise, every person who has accepted Jesus Christ as Lord has the Holy Spirit living within. But that does not mean that he or she is filled with the Spirit, and empowered for service.

Think about what great exploits some have done for the Lord without being filled with the Holy Spirit and speaking in tongues. Now imagine what they may have accomplished if they had that added dimension of power, the ability to operate in the supernatural, endued with power from on High. WOW.

According to the sacred Scriptures, when we are baptized with the Holy Ghost and speak in tongues, we enter into another level in God. And through praying daily in this supernatural language of the Spirit, we can tap into more and more of God's Presence and His power.

Praying in tongues is a treasure, because the Bible teaches that when we pray in the Spirit, we are speaking directly to God, and speaking mysteries. This means that the devil cannot understand what we are saying to our wonderful Heavenly Father, Jehovah God.

We are talking to Him in such intimate and marvelous terms that it is spirit to Spirit, by the Holy Spirit.

Here are four things that praying in tongues will do for your spiritual life and walk with Almighty God"

1. Praying in tongues will enable you to have private conversations with Almighty God, which neither man nor devil can hinder or understand.

2. Praying in tongues, as the Spirit gives you the words will enable you to draw closer to God the Father than ever before and pray concerning His plan and purpose for your life.

3. Praying in other tongues will enable you to pray about situations, circumstances and other people, who needs your prayers, but about which you may have no natural knowledge.

4. Praying in other tongues will build up your born again human spirit and make you spiritually strong. You will develop spiritual muscles and if you persist in praying in the Holy Ghost and never give up, you will become a mighty force for God in the earth. You will experience and operate in His power.

To receive the baptism with the Holy Spirit, with the evidence of praying in other tongues just pray this simple prayer and mean it with all of your heart: Lord Jesus Christ. I believe You are the Son of God. You are my Savior and my Lord. You are the One Who baptizes with the Holy Ghost and with Fire. Fill me with Your Spirit. Fill me to over-flowing. And, according to your Word, let the Holy Spirit give me the supernatural language of tongues so that I can communicate with the Father, spirit to Spirit. I receive the baptism with the Holy

Ghost right now, in Jesus Name, thank You that I am now filled, and fully expect to speak with other tongues as they did in the Holy Bible, all throughout the Book of Acts. In Jesus Name I pray, and believe that I receive. Amen.

Now thank and praise Him. The language will come. Speak it out. And once it begins, pray in the supernatural language daily. You will be glad you did.

MOVE OF THE HOLY SPIRIT

"The Writings of a Stiff Necked Unteachable Reprobate" such were the errors put forth recently by a false messenger and blasphemer on my blog with regard to the above mentioned subject. If ever there was an example of "Majoring in the Minors", to compound his errors, then this is it, and make no mistake.

However, let's deal with first things first. What does this expression mean i.e. "A Move of The Holy Spirit?" I ask this, because it's a favourite jargon term of the "Next New Experience Trick" and/or "What shall we do this month to keep 'em occupied and happy" Charismatic branches of the Cainite-Judeo-Christian Religion. These charlatans love their so called "moves of the spirit" but are they moves of The Holy Spirit? I, regrettably, have been in their company in the past when these so called 'moves' are supposed to have taken place. I tell you, folks, I am not the least bit convinced at all that these things are or were the works of The Holy Spirit, a spirit YES, but not The Holy Spirit. But what of

this term "A Move of The Holy Spirit", where does it come from and is it Scriptural?

Yes it is Scriptural, but only just by a gnat's whisker, chuckle chuckle. Here it is, in the only place it can be found in the Holy Scriptures:

2 Peter 1:21 (KJV) For the prophecy came not in old time by the will of man: but Holy men of God spake as they were moved by The Holy Ghost (Spirit). (Brackets and emphasis mine)

So what is this 'moving' of the Holy Spirit all about? Well it's simple isn't it, in the above Scriptural scenario it's a prompting by The Holy Spirit to speak out and say something, and in this case it's to prophesy - well these guys were prophets, so what do we expect - silence? But does this expression relate or apply to anything else, say a healing or someone babbling away with a load of Charismatic gobbledegook? No, it doesn't. Healing is a gift of The Holy Spirit and if you are fortunate enough to have this gift then The Holy Spirit will work

through you and you will heal people as and when the opportunity arises. Once indwelled by the Holy Spirit you can use that Power as and when, not wait for a movement.

Likewise with tongues, if you need to communicate with someone of a foreign tongue or there is someone present to interpret your Spiritual tongue then just get on with it. On these occasions, there will be no special 'moves' of the Holy Spirit as suggested by our commentator, you, with that gift, will heal people just as Peter did. Whether it will be your shadow that heals or not I cannot say. Now am I splitting hairs here? No way, because our commentator does not believe in the indwelling of The Holy Spirit so he, and please note this, without The Holy Spirit is always waiting for the next 'move' to take place, like someone waiting for a bus at a bus stop before he does something. It's as if he cannot do anything until his spiritual bus turns up and he hops on. Laughable or what?

So what does this tell us? It tells us he's not birthed in God, he has no understanding of what it means to be Born of God (Born Again). This also tells us he has no understanding of what takes place at Baptism, and yet he had the audacity to say this:

"The best advice I can leave you with is to make an appointment with your doctor and ask him or her to refer you for evaluation with a psychiatric specialist. I come from a medical family and know these people are generally pretty good at what they do."

Cheeky eh? but these two sentences reveal much. 1) He blasphemously accuses me of being insane (this in itself is a blasphemy against The Holy Spirit) and 2) He shows his faith in the secular and worldly medical profession and yet boasts of moves of The Spirit when he claims he has healed someone. Is this double mindedness? You bet, and why would a Spirit empowered healer express faith in the medical profession? Something to hold in the back of our minds whilst I press on.

I will also add that being accused of being insane is very encouraging, because they said the same thing about Yashua Messiah:

John 10:20 (KJV) And many of them said, He hath a devil, and is mad; why hear ye Him? (Emphasis mine)

Back to the subject at hand and a ☐uestion. If this topic of 'moves of the Spirit' is so important, why did Yashua Messiah only mention it ONCE in His Holy Scriptures? If it was so important why not mention it at least as many times as Grace i.e. 170 times in 159 verses of The Holy Scriptures. This alone should tell us what is important to Yashua Messiah.

However, for the sake of this discussion if we look up the word 'healed' in the New Testament we find it mentioned 46 times in 45 verses and I have been through them without finding the term: "moved in The Spirit" ONCE!!! in relation to healing. So what does this tell us? It tells us that these sensationalist gimmicky 'when and where's the next new experience going to happen' types have misappropriated the term:

"Moved by The Holy Ghost (Spirit)" from Peter's letter and are miss-using or misapplying it to build a circus show of tricks in order to build a BELIEF SYSTEM!!! Interesting term eh? It's one of his and here we get our commentator's use of it:

"I am therefore not using religious jargon but speak from direct experience of covenant relationship with the Father through Jesus their reciprocating via the Holy Spirit, if that fits your belief system."

Notice, "Covenant relationship". Do I sense a touch of The Old Covenant Law in operation there somewhere rather than The New Covenant? We shall see. He then denies he is using religious jargon without even realising he has done that very thing by the misappropriation of the term 'moved by The Spirit'. Have you noticed something else? It's as if he's doing The Father a favour. LOL. HE is favouring THEM with his agreement via The New Covenant, not THEM blessing him via that same New Covenant - THEY are reciprocating after he has done them a favour!! This thinking is based solely on the corrupt: "I have accepted a 'Jesus' as my saviour" nonsense.

Furthermore, what is a Belief SYSTEM? How can a heart felt Belief in Yashua Messiah ever be a systematic or methodical belief system? Here's a Dictionary definition or three from Dictionary.com:

1) Having, showing, or involving a system, method, or plan: 2) given to or using a system or method; methodical: 3) arranged in or comprising an ordered system.

I mean, come on, who would use such ridiculous terminology other than a Spiritually devoid Bible intellectual? He must have written this stuff when he was at the bus stop waiting for his next 'move of the Spirit' after having put on his managing director's suit or army uniform. More mirth for the author.

Having got this far, I must now return to the beginning of our discussion when he came onto my blog in answer to this point that I had made to another visitor:

"No it's not possible for a BELIEVER to commit the unpardonable sin, only ex-believers, who turn their backs on Yashua Messiah. This would then mean them turning against Him and in so doing blaspheming against The Holy Spirit that He sends to us at the point of our Baptism and Spiritual gifting."

Here is his Question:

"Or could this be one who thinks they believe in Jesus but reject Him by rejecting a move of the Holy Spirit?"

Straight away we can see his obsession with this Cainite-Judeo-Christian Charismatic Religious humbug of moves of a spirit. Not only that, but we also have him judging others whom he pigeon holes as those who only THINK they believe in Yashua Messiah. I mean, who does he think he is? How arrogant, judgemental and self-righteous can you get? Has it even dawned on him that these people may be right and have sussed him out with his mickey mouse obsession re moves of a spirit, and

he is wrong? I doubt whether the thought has ever crossed his mind.

WAYS TO ENJOY THE HOLY SPIRIT'S PRESENCE IN CORPORATE SETTINGS

To have the privilege of enjoying the Holy Spirit's presence, we must first understand that Jesus left Him on earth to be the leader, the guide, and Comforter to the Church. The more we know about the Holy Spirit; His role in assisting the Church, and His role in our personal lives, the greater we will see His manifestations in our individual lives, as well as when we come together as a group--corporately.

When we come together in a corporate setting, for corporate praise, worship, prayer, preaching, bible study, or whatever the purpose: The scriptures says where there is two or more, gathered together in the name of Jesus that the Holy Spirit is in the midst. But before He will manifest Himself (demonstrate that He is present), there must be a certain atmosphere created for Him to show up.

I've listed fourteen things I've learned during my almost thirty years in ministry on how to create an atmosphere for the Holy Spirit to move in our services. This relates to corporate praise and worship--not private devotion.

- Before beginning any service, there should be one person who is recognized or designated by the group as the leader of praise and worship. This is important because every time God's people come together, someone must take the lead. The Holy Spirit honors authority and leadership. Why? Because it was ordained by God the Father. The Holy Spirit understands His place within the Godhead and He works within the authority God has given Him. He will not usurp His or any one else's authority. He seeks no praise or worship for Himself, only that believers will praise and worship God the Father and Jesus Christ, the Son.
- Recognize that anytime God's people (2 or 3) gather together in the name of Jesus, He is automatically there in

the midst. Even though He is there, He will not automatically manifest Himself unless He is asked to do so.

- Once we realize He is present, we must recognize and honor His presence.
- Invite Him to come into the service and ask that His will be done in the service. This is necessary because the Holy Spirit is a gentleman. He is very sensitive and will not stay any where that He is not welcomed or wanted. He will not force His will on any person. He will show up but will not manifest Himself; only if He is asked or invited to do so. If He becomes grieved, He will leave. That's why there are spiritual gatherings where no matter how spiritual one may be, you may not be able to sense His presence. That's because the right atmosphere has not been set for Him to manifest Himself. If the Holy Spirit becomes grieved by the leadership or by what is going on in that setting, He will leave and you will not sense His presence. Again, He always shows up when two or more believers come

together in the name of Jesus, but He will not always manifest Himself; for the reasons I have indicated.

- Once the stage is set, by inviting Him into the service, everyone should begin to praise and worship Jesus Christ together. The Holy Spirit wants us to exalt the name of Jesus; that name that is above every name. Unless there is a praise and worship team or a worship leader designated to lead the service, the one who will lead the Body into corporate worship may not have emerged, as yet. He or she is worshipping as part of the group--the corporate body.

- In the beginning of praise and worship; before sensing the presence of the Holy Spirit; you may sense dryness in your words. The words being spoken to the Lord may feel lifeless; like the Lord is not hearing you; you may feel like your words are not going up to heaven but are just bouncing off the ceiling. This is because your mind and carnal thoughts need to be cleansed and your carnal thoughts must be transformed into spiritual thoughts. Do not give up and do not despair at this point because this is the phase where you are moving from the flesh/carnal realm into the spirit realm. Sometimes, it may take a while for the group, or even the leader to break through this realm into the spirit realm, and get on one accord. Just keep praising and worshipping God, and exalting the name of Jesus. Keep talking to Him and telling Him how much you love Him; how wonderful He is and so on. This is where a strong praise and worship leader, a minister, or someone who has been fasting and praying is very important. He or she will keep pressing through the fleshly/carnal realm and into the spirit realm with words of praise and thanksgiving to God until there is a breakthrough where the presence of God begins to illuminate the lead worshipper, and the other worshippers. At this point, every one who has tapped into the spiritual realm begins to sense that God is

hearing their words of praise and thanksgiving.

- By now, the praise and worship leader should have taken the lead and began to lead all others into songs, psalms, words of exhortation, prayer, prophecy, and so on. Now, everyone should be encouraged to talk to and to express their personal feelings to the Lord. As an example, you might be instructed to tell Him how wonderful He is; how marvelous He is, how much you love Him; how you depend on Him and without Him you can do nothing. If you don't know what to say, follow the words of the worship leader, or you can prepare a head of time, by reading the Psalms of one of the most famous worship leaders of all times--King David. Write down some of the words, statements, and songs King David, the shepherd, the warrior, or the servant, used to worship and magnify the Lord. You may just want to read words of expression to God, directly out of the Bible. The purpose of this is to get your mind on spiritual things and in

touch with God. In general worship, the Holy Spirit will respond when we sing from our hearts, songs to God and Jesus-not songs about Them. It is very important that we sing to Him in praise and worship, and not about Him. This will bring His presence into a room quicker than anything. We see this when David sang and played his harp before King Saul. The anointed music brought the presence of God and drove the evil spirits from Saul's presence. David was a minstrel and this is the work of a minstrel.

- During this time of corporate praise and worship, the anointing of the Holy Spirit will begin to rest upon one person in the group (this may or may not be the praise and worship leader). Whoever the anointing falls upon, that person should take the lead in continuing to praise and worship by leading the group as far into the Spirit of oneness, as possible. The objective is to get everyone on one accord. The leader may change from one person to another, during the course of general praise and worship, or it may

be one person throughout the entire time who takes the lead and brings the group into the spirit of oneness. All of this is done in unity...decently...and in order and without confusion.

- When the group has moved from the carnal or fleshly realm into the spirit realm, everyone will be on one accord and should be sensing or feeling the presence of the Holy Spirit. Again, this sensing of His presence occurs through personal praise and worship, by telling the Lord how much you love Him: in general, just praising Him with personal words of love, gratitude and admiration, or by singing songs to Him and not songs about Him. One by one, as the group senses the presence of the Holy Spirit, that's when pure praise and worship begins to take place, and the Holy Spirit's presence gets stronger and stronger. At this time more and more people will begin to sense His presence.
- Once the group is on one accord, pure praise and worship is now going up to the throne of God - to God the Father.

In John 4:23-24 Jesus said, "The hour cometh, and now is, when the true worshippers shall worship the Father in spirit and in truth: for the Father seeketh such to worship him. God is a Spirit: and they that worship him must worship him in spirit and in truth." Hopefully, every one in the group is now sensing the presence of the Holy Spirit on some level. Pure praise and worship is now going forward. The presence of God/the Holy Spirit should be strong at this point. This level of praise and worship will continue until the Holy Spirit begins moving upon the worship leader, or the minster to shift from corporate praise and worship to another direction in the now spirit-filled service. At this time one person in the group--the pastor, apostle, elder, prophet, evangelist, teacher, musician, or so on, should be anointed to take the lead and begin to flow in the Spirit through continued praise, worship, songs, prayer, or some other manifestations of the Spirit.

- When the group is on one accord that's when the Holy Spirit's presence is the strongest. So, the greater the unity in the group, the stronger the presence of the God the Holy Spirit. The more divided the group; the weaker the presence of the Holy Spirit. If there is lots of bitterness and contention among the group, it's very unlikely that you will sense His presence in a tangible way.

- When the presence of the Holy Spirit is strong in a group, and almost everyone is sensing the presence of God; He begins to search the people's hearts for faith. When the He finds faith, He will begin to move upon the person with faith for him or her to ask God for whatever is on their heart. That person or persons will begin to sense the personal ministry of the Holy Spirit. The stronger the group's faith, the greater the manifestation of the Holy Spirit will be both corporately and individually. As the Holy Spirit begins to minister personally to those in the service there may be manifestations of joy, shouting,

dancing, weeping, kneeling in worship or so on. If there is corporate faith for a certain need, the Holy Spirit will begin to inspire someone who is anointed to minister in that area. The Holy Spirit may begin to move upon one person or persons in the group, based on their individual anointings (abilities). That's when one or more of the nine gifts of the Holy Spirit may begin to operate: The gifts of divers tongues, interpretation of tongues, prophecy; the gifts of the word of wisdom, the word of knowledge, the discerning of spirits; the gifts of faith, working of miracles and healings may begin to manifest. These are the nine gifts of the Spirit (1Corinthians 12:1-11).

- The Holy Spirit manifests Himself through the nine gifts of the Spirit based on the knowledge and maturity level of the believers present. If pure faith, and dependency solely upon God is demonstrated, He will work miracles regardless of the maturity and knowledge of the believers. He is hindered from the greatest

manifestations if there is unbelief and doubt in the group. The greater the doubt and unbelief, the less He will manifest Himself. The more faith and knowledge of the Word of God is present, the greater the manifestation of His Spirit and Presence, and the greater the signs, wonders, miracles, and answers to prayer.

- He responds □uickly to praise and worship that exalts Jesus Christ; and particularly to anointed music that is played and sang to glorify God and not the one singing or playing the instruments.

There are too many church services where the Holy Spirit's presence is not welcomed or not understood. As believers in Christ, we should welcome His presence in our midst--after all Jesus said He would not leave us here comfortless but was going to send the Holy Spirit to carry on His work after He ascended back to heaven.

THE HOLINESS THAT COMES THROUGH FIRE

Have you been surprised by something strange recently? Peter says not to be surprised at the fiery ordeal among us, the fiery trials that come upon us to test us, as though some strange thing is happening to us **(I Pet. 4:12).** Yet we realize why he warned us not to be surprised because it seems that is always our tendency. "What's going on?" we cry. "Where did this come from?"

No one likes hard times. And life can sometimes be quite challenging, even for Christians. Peter goes on to say that we should rejoice to the degree that we share the sufferings of Christ, in other words, being reviled for the name of Jesus, persecuted for righteousness sake **(I Pet. 4:13-16).** And indeed, when we are walking in the perfect will of God, this is the only kind of suffering that we should endure. After all, Jesus' sacrifice of 33 and a half years included every kind of suffering that Satan brings upon us such as sickness,

rejection, the result of curses, including the curse of poverty on the last day of His life. He was a substitutionary sacrifice for us. He suffered in our place so we don't have to suffer these attacks of Satan. The reality, however, is that we do not always walk in God's perfect will. Sometimes we suffer because of a lack of knowledge.

One of our pastors in Africa just lost his daughter in death. This is one of the greatest trials parents can face. But God's promise is that no test will be too great for us to bear because He is always with us **(I Cor. 10:13).** Even when we find ourselves obliged to walk for a spell through the valley of the shadow of death, we can reach out for the hand of our Shepherd Jesus to lead us through that valley. His rod and His staff do indeed comfort us **(Psalm 23).** No matter what we go through, He promised that He would always be there as Yahovah Shammah. He would never leave us or forsake us, even when it seemed like He did **(Heb. 13:5).** It is in those times of fiery trials that we realize that our God who is Love is more concerned with our holy character that will

last forever than with the ease we may experience in a trouble-free life. Not that He brings the fire upon us directly. Satan does that. But God is the overall orchestrator of the process of purification that results.

Even Jesus Learned Through Suffering

Here is where we come to the gist of this message - the concept of holiness by fire. And we must not say that fiery trials only come to the imperfect. Jesus never sinned. Yet He grew up as a young child who needed to grow in His Father's character of love. The Word says: "Although He was a Son, He learned obedience from the things which He suffered. And having been made perfect, He became to all those who obey Him the source of eternal salvation, being designated by God as a high priest according to the order of Melchizedek" **(Heb. 5:8-10).** While the joy of Jesus was without a doubt in Jesus Himself, He was also called a man of suffering or a "man of sorrows and ac□uainted with grief" **(Isa. 63:3).**

He went through every type of trial we face in order to be a compassionate Intercessor or Go-between with our Father in heaven **(Heb.4:14-15).** He knows. He knows exactly what we're going through. He is interceding for us every step of the way. And the Holy Spirit is the One our "Father of mercies and God of all comfort" **(II Cor. 1:3)** sent to go alongside us to comfort and encourage us **(John 14:26).** Jesus is the Word, and He has a part as well. He holds our hand and like a faithful Shepherd gives us a place to rest in green pastures even in the midst of the valley of trial. Jesus' Word is always there. There is a verse for every hurt, every trial, "so that through perseverance and the encouragement of the Scriptures we might have hope." And as this verse continues in **Romans 15:4-5**, "Now may the God who gives perseverance and encouragement grant you to be of the same mind with one another according to Christ Jesus."

Holiness: Being in Agreement with the God who is Love

That is the essence of holiness: being of the same mind as Jesus Christ. Agreeing in everything with God is the central meaning of holiness. Thinking, speaking, and doing exactly like our perfect Father Love - that is holiness. And a definite link exists with the concept of fire - the trial of fire we go through. Songs about revival fire notwithstanding, fire does not revive. Fire cleanses and purifies. Fire burns out bad habits. Fire destroys that which is not love in us. Our goal is be exactly like our Father Love. Praise and worship is important in that journey, but it is not the goal. The goal is be like Love. The goal is to be defined as Love as God is defined.

Love is the definition of God. God is Love **(I John 4:8).** He tells us to be holy like He is holy -- to be Love like He is Love. He is eternally defined as Love. Paul tells us to "imitators of God" and to "walk in love," abstaining from impurity "as is proper among saints" **(Eph. 5:1-3).** A saint is defined as a holy one. A holy one is one in whom the Holy One, God, dwells, but also one who allows God to work in them to make them more and more like their

Father, who is Love. Love defines God, and love should define us. Because our souls and bodies, however, have not come in perfect agreement yet with our spirits, we need "re-fining" in order to be "de-fined" as love. We shall see shortly how those words are part of the root of the word holy.

Jesus also is eternally defined as Love. Jesus came down into this space we call time, however, to grow up from a young child and to bring the concept of holiness to a new level. In another sense, He came to bring holiness down to our level. It is in His journey on earth that we find the meaning of the word holy in a number of languages. The root ho has the meaning of refine and define. Jesus was refined by the fire of trial in His life so that He would show us the way in all things and in all trials to be refined from all that is not love to be finally defined like our Father - defined as Love. Because sin entered the world through Adam and because we are surrounded by a world of sin, it became an inevitable necessity for us to be refined by fiery trial. As metals are assayed or purged from impurities to become pure metals, so we are tested through fire to eliminate all impurities and be refined so that we can ultimately be defined as Love. Pure, unadulterated love. No fear, because there is no fear in love. There is no insecurity in love. There is no pride in love. There is no lust, no selfishness in love.

Peter states the concept clearly. After stressing the importance of the salvation ready to be revealed in the last time, He writes in **I Peter 1:6-7,** "In this [in Yashua's salvation] you greatly rejoice, even though now for a little while [alas, sometimes that little while does not seem like a little while, but in view of eternity it is indeed a short time], if necessary [sometimes we can be refined simply by reading the Word of God, allowing ourselves to be chastened by the Word, as **Psalm 94:12 shows],** you have been distressed by various trials, so that the proof of your faith, being more precious than gold which is perishable, even though tested by fire, may be found to result in praise and glory and honor at the revelation of Jesus Christ."

Spirits Perfect, Souls Not

Our spirits are perfect, but our souls, our hearts, minds, and wills need purifying. As Jeremiah said, "Yet, O [Eternal] of hosts, You who test [not tempt] the righteous, Who see the mind and the heart..." **(Jer. 20:12).** So it is the mind and heart that need the testing, not the spirit. And notice that God tests the righteous. Righteousness is a legal standing before God. We have a right to be seen as righteous and perfect in our spirits because of the precious blood of Jesus. God calls us, the perfect "us "in our spirits, the righteousness of God in Christ Jesus **(II Cor. 5:21).**

We need to understand the shade of difference between our standing in righteousness before a holy God and what it really means to be holy. As we grow to sin less and less, we are agreeing more and more with God's way of thinking. We are agreeing with Him. We are being refined by trials and by the Word of God becoming a part of us, and we are progressively being more and more defined as God is defined - defined as Love, perfect Love. This is not to

discourage us, because even when we fall into sin, which God always foreknows, our need for Jesus is made more real. We recognize our total dependence on Him and our need for His blood to cleanse us. All things, yes, even the sins we stumble into, work for our good **(Rom. 8:28; Gen. 50:20).** We always learn lessons when we sin and get up and keep on going, declaring every day a new day with new mercies in it **(II Cor. 4:16).**

Increased opposition to the truth, including curses from major organizations and many wrong prayers have recently caused attacks on the physical bodies of the leadership of Freedom Church of God. These attacks have brought me understanding of the difference between godly suffering and suffering God does not desire for us. Persecution for righteousness and truth is in fact the only kind of suffering in which God tells us to rejoice **(I Pet. 4:12-16).** So I rejoice in being persecuted for the truth, since Jesus said that meant I was truly a son of God **(Mat. 5:10-12, 44-45).** On the other hand, I do hate the attack of persistent pain and continue to thank Jesus that this too will pass as greater revelation is received, and I thank Him for the freedom from pain and the ability to sleep. We must hate the things God hates, and He hates any attack on our bodies or souls that Jesus paid for, while He is pleased to see us rejoice in persecution for the sake of Jesus' name and walk in His forgiveness of our enemies.

Fire of the Word Not Enough

God compares His Word to a fire **(Jer. 23:39).** If we were perfect, that would be the only fire we need to purify us. We would be chastened only by God's Word **(Ps. 94:12).** It would be great if all of us allowed ourselves to be corrected and purified solely be reading and studying the Word of God. But God foreknew that such a scenario would simply not exist. That's why He sent Jesus to die for us, and to live a sacrificial life for over thirty years to show us the example of overcoming -- at times through suffering.

That is why the Father appointed Jesus to purify His fellow priests, which we are, by

fire. Malachi prophesies a time of increased fire of purification that will exist at the beginning of the Millennium to purify the physical priests of Levi. But millennial prophecy has overlaps. It includes the last days just before the coming back of Jesus. We know that these times of tribulation and Great Tribulation are times of severe trial, even for believers. **Malachi 3:2-3** says, "But who can endure the day of His coming? And who can stand when He appears? For He is like a refiner's fire [remember that the root of the word holy includes the meaning of "refine"] and like fullers' soap. He will sit as a smelter and purifier of silver, and He will purify the sons of Levi and refine them like gold and silver, so that they may present to the [Eternal] offerings in righteousness."

The Smelting Analogy Applies to End-time Preparation for the Rapture

Smelting was an important process in the ancient world. Fire separated precious metals from ore and inferior metals. This process became the analogy of divine testing. Gold and silver became symbols of

God's work of perfection of character in our lives, while by products such as lead and copper became symbols of dead works. Fire assaying in which the □uality of a metal was proven and impurities called dross were removed became a symbol showing how God allows fiery trials to prove our worth and make us pure or completely holy, dedicated fully to God.

Proverbs 17:3 states the process succinctly: "The refining pot is for silver and the furnace for gold, But the [Eternal] tests [bachan, perform a □ualification test, acceptance test; validate; proof test; assay] hearts." God calls His ministers a flame of fire **(Heb. 1:7)** as they speak out God's fiery Word. God told young Jeremiah, using the same word, bachan, "I have made you an assayer and a tester among My people, That you may know and assay their way" **(Jer. 6:27).** Once again, the millennial prophecy of holiness by fire will have its precursor in these last days: "It will come about that he who is left in Zion and remains in Jerusalem will be called holy - everyone who is recorded for life in Jerusalem. When the [Eternal] has washed

away the filth of the daughters of Zion and purged the bloodshed of Jerusalem from her midst, by the spirit of judgment and the spirit of burning [ba`ar or testing by fire]" **(Isa. 4:3-4).** We see in this last verse that those who stand the test by fire are called holy - an accurate reflection of the root ho - refined and thus defined, tested and found true to the definition of God, which is love.

God showed Daniel what would happen in "the end time" **(Dan. 12:9-10):** "Many will be purged, purified and refined [made holy or in greater and greater agreement with God and His character of love]...." That refining process has already begun, and the process will get hotter and hotter as Jesus' return approaches. Those who allow the process of holiness by fire to have its perfect work in their lives now will be the ones who persevere and escape the Great Tribulation by the first and best rapture **(Mat. 24:12-13; Luke 21:36; Isa.26:20-21).** The days of the rapture are here. That's the title of a future book we are planning that we hope comes out before the rapture. Being ready for the rapture will

re□uire some fire. In Paul's letter that spoke much about the rapture, he gives the key to being ready: "Now may the God of peace [shalom or wholeness] sanctify [make you holy, set apart totally for Him to be like Him in every way] you entirely; and may your spirit and soul and body be preserved complete, without blame at the coming of our [Divine Master] Jesus Christ. Faithful is He who calls you, and He also will bring it to pass" **(I Thes. 5:23-24).**

More Definitions of Holiness

At this point we need to more fully understand the concept of holiness, of which a number of definitions exist. The ground Moses stood on in Exodus 3 was called holy ground. Why? Because God's presence was in it. We are holy and the Sabbath is holy for the same reason. Furthermore, if God is in us and in the Sabbath, we and God's day are set apart or sanctified, set aside for a special, holy use. We and God's day are devoted or dedicated to God. Not all of us have a name like my daughter Lisa. Lisa comes from Elizabeth, which comes from the Hebrew and means

"consecrated to God." Bethel was a place name that meant, "house of God." Whatever our name may be, when Jesus comes to live in us, we become holy, set apart for God.

The concept of purity is included, since God cannot live in an impure vessel. The day into which Jesus pours Himself becomes pure and holy. The day is purely dedicated to Jesus and to no other temporal use. We are also called to be set apart for the pure purposes of God. Our souls must begin to reflect the purity and perfect dedication of our spirits. The nation of Israel (as are the believers today) were called to be "holy unto God" - devoted only to Him. We are to be true to Him and have no competing loyalties. God calls Himself holy because He is true to Himself. He is faithful and perfectly true to His Word. He does not lie to others or to Himself. He is faithful and consistent in His words, character, and actions. In a word, He has integrity. The three members of the Godhead are perfectly integrated, perfectly united in themselves and true to themselves and each other.

We are also to be true to God and ourselves - One with ourselves and God as the Father, Son, and Holy Spirit are One, in perfect unity and faithfulness. Like God, we are to do what we say, to fulfill our promises, to be the same in private as in public. I'm sure we could give many reasons why David was a man after God's own heart **(Acts 13:22).** One of them is revealed in one of his psalms: "I will give heed to the blameless way [margin: way of integrity]...I will walk within my house in the integrity of my heart. I will set no worthless thing before my eyes [even when no one is looking]..." **(Ps. 101:3-4).** Someone once said that integrity is what you are and do in the dark. And God will bring to light all that is in the dark. God will bring into judgment "everything which is hidden" (Eccl. 12:14) unless it is confessed and erased by the blood of Jesus.

A Lesson from Midian

Jesus commanded Israel to execute His vengeance on the Midianites. They made war with them and killed many of them,

burning their cities and camps in order to purify the land from their uncleanness **(Numb. 31:11).** The warriors had to purify themselves from the uncleanness, including the touching of any dead bodies **(31:19).** All the metal that had been used in battle, "everything that can stand the fire, you shall pass through the fire, and it shall be clean..." **(31:23).** The uncleanness was burned out of the metals by fire, just as our uncleanness is burned out by fiery trials. Jesus speaks of the "fire of His jealousy" **(Zeph. 1:18).**

He wants to burn out of us anything that competes with our wholehearted, holy devotion to Him. As the metals of battle were purified by fire and also by water, the psalmist says, "We went through fire and water, Yet You brought us out into a place of abundance" **(Ps. 66:12).** The fiery trials God allows us sometimes to go through are for our ultimate good. Satan and people may mean it for evil, but Jesus always has a plan of redemption **(Gen. 50:20).** It surely feels good when the pain is over and the trial has passed, and we enter our large place of green pastures, our place of abundance. The eternal good that the trial produced, however, could not have been obtained without the fire.

In these last days it is the intensity of the fire that will be the question. Those who persist in the lackadaisical, nonchalant attitude of the Laodicean era will have to buy "gold refined by fire" **(Rev. 3:18)** in the Great Tribulation. On the other hand, those who are obedient to Jesus and who persevere through their fiery trials will be spared from the "hour of testing ... to test those who dwell on the earth" **(Rev. 3:10).** The day is coming, and in some cases is already here, when "each man's work will become evident; for the day will show it because it is to revealed with fire, and the fire itself will test the □uality of each man's work" **(I Cor. 3:14).**

What will be our final fire? The fire of the Word that corrects us and the fiery trials that test our metal as we persevere faithfully to be counted worthy to escape all these things and stand before the Son of Man in heaven after we are raptured ? Or will it be the fire of the Great Tribulation

that will make or break us and force us to lose our lives to gain the reward? What will be our choice? We pray that we will all persevere in trial as did Job, and that His words in **Job 23:10** will become ours: "But He knows the way I take; When He has tried me, I shall come forth as gold."